Published in 2012
Written by Julian Hall

ISBN-10: 1477583211
Cover design by Jeremy Salmon
© Julian Hall 2012

DEDICATIONS

This book is dedicated to entrepreneurs everywhere working around the clock. Missing out on drinks withfriends and bedtime stories with their kids.
But in the end you change our lives for the better, sometimes forever.
Your examples have made me live a life more free.
Keep being.

A special dedication goes to my children - baby boy Malachi, my heartbeat Na'ariyah, genius Akir, prince Shalmuwn and Zakariyah the boss.

ACKNOWLEDGMENTS

I also want to thank my wife for keeping the green smoothies coming and the oxtail cooking, Leah Salmon for sense checking everything, Nadia Maddy for helping me see the potential in this book, Eunice Nisbett for the book marketing plan, Jacqueline Asafu-Adjaye for the about the aauthor image, Mark Lewis for the book trailer, Jeremy Salmon for being probably the best designer ever, my Father for always being there at the drop of a hat and my Mother for giving me everything she had.

Preface

Entrepreneurship as we know it today has become a way of life, religious even. People worship the ground that successful entrepreneurs walk on, hang off their every word and try to work out what makes them different. It's clear that really successful entrepreneurs are more than just business people. You only have to speak to one for a short time to realise that most have a philosophical and almost spiritual outlook on life. Their journey as entrepreneurs has done more than just increase their bank balance. It has led them down a road of self discovery; a road of seeming enlightenment for which they are forever grateful. You see them at the pulpits of entrepreneurship - giving back at seminars, lectures and workshops and offering words of wisdom and experience to those aspiring entrepreneurs.

It would appear that many of them truly want to make a real difference to something or someone in this world. Sure, money is a motivator but not a full stop for them and the cash is almost a by-product of the value they bring. They have given us ideas, solutions and technologies which have in many cases irreversibly changed the world forever. They have enriched the lives of millions through communication, education, information, social enterprise, media and so much more. It almost feels like the world's consciousness is working through them to answer the problems we face and help us evolve. Never before has there been a greater need for problem solvers in a world which appears to have more problems than ever.

So are entrepreneurs the new sages or wise men? Are they the vessels through which a divine force works to deliver a message or a solution? I don't know. However, I do know that it is surely a new day and time, where the ink doesn't dry on the page of reality for very long. Change is around us constantly; changes we could have never predicted or imagined. Thanks to those visionary men and women we call entrepreneurs. They chase every innovation, find solutions to every problem and change the game every day of our lives.

It is my suggestion dear reader that it's no longer fair to call these individuals simply entrepreneurs. I think they've become more than that, I think they have become what I call, **Ultrapreneurs.**
Here are my definitions of these terms:

Ultrapreneur
Someone who has exceeded in their undertaking as an entrepreneur but also has a profound effect on their family, community, country or humanity.

Ultrapreneurship
A holistic approach encompassing all aspects of one's life including entrepreneurship, health and well being, family, spirituality, morality and mentality which come together to provide supreme balance.

As I look back and reflect on the lessons I have learned on the road called entrepreneurship I humbly share with you 100 sayings, lessons, thoughts and ideas of my own.

I can guarantee, that if you follow these, not only will you surpass your goals but you'll achieve them quicker than you expected. And more importantly you will contribute to the world becoming a better place.
It's my hope that at least one of these sayings will make you sit back and realise what you're doing or what you're not doing. It's intended to be read quickly but thought about for a long time. Those thoughts I hope will inspire you to take action then act on something, anything!

So for those who aspire to be, for those who are and for those on the road to becoming Ultrapreneurs, "I give you the little I have ...in the hope that it will be the little you need."

Julian Hall

"**Be** passionate about your business …not emotional"

"**Just** because you build it…doesn't mean they'll come"

"**Change** isn't just constant…it's necessary"

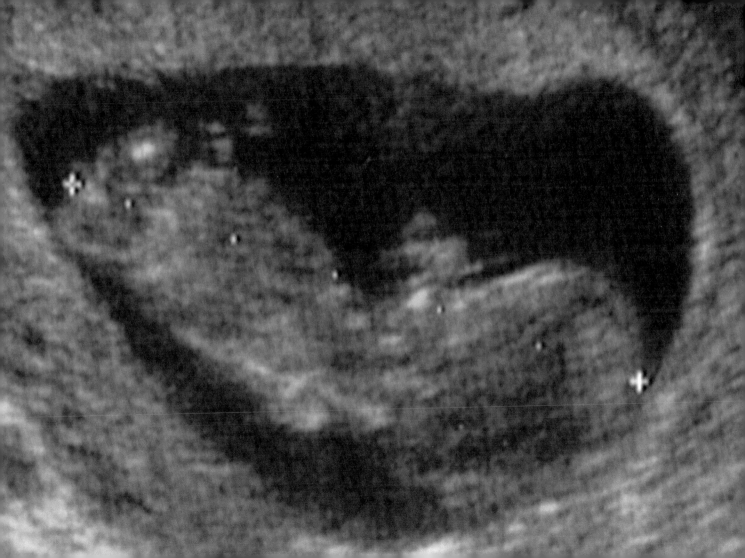

"**Why** compete, when you can…create"

"**If** you stay ready…you don't have to get ready"

"**Overcome** your overwhelm…and overachieve"

"**If** you want more…give more"

"**If** business is war…then integrity is honour"

"**Good** people make a system work…great people make a system better"

"**Know** what entrepreneurship means…to you"

"**If** you chase the money…it
will keep running"

"**Cowardice** is…conformity"

"**Have** you proven your…business model?"

"**Money** isn't scarce…amazing ideas are"

Fourteen

"**Go** smart…or go home"

"**Critical** mass is vanity…monetizing is sanity"

"**Are** your business partners…working as hard as you?"

Seventeen

"**Vision** boards means nothing…if your vision doesn't make sense"

"**If** they get in the way of your dream…make sure it's not a nightmare"

Nineteen

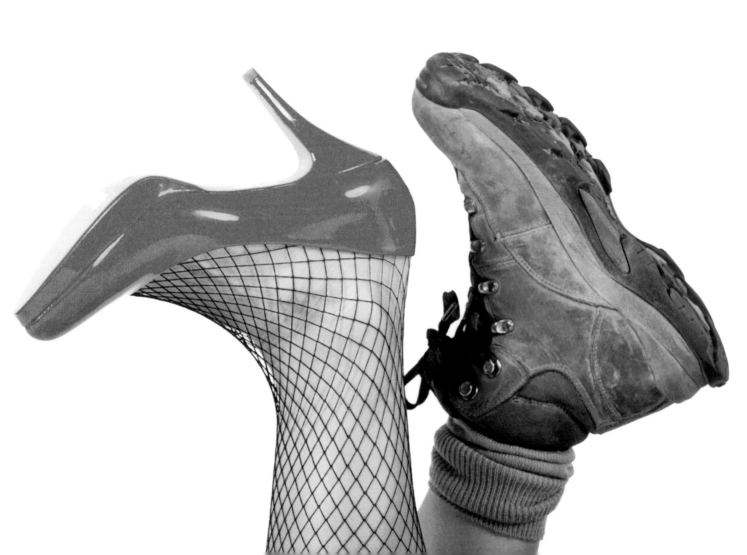

"**Ultrapreneurs** and business people...are not the same thing"

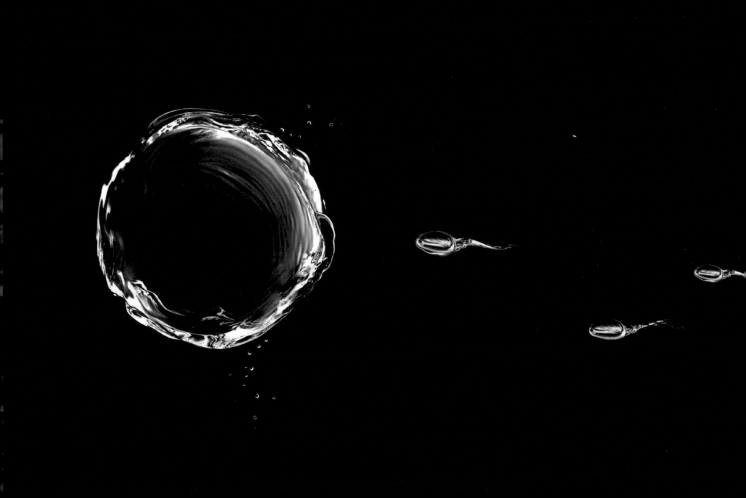

"**One** bad ass idea…is better than
ten on the shelf"

Twenty One

"**Ultrapreneuship** is an undertaking…but don't let it take you under"

Twenty Two

"**Failure** is a good thing…just not all the time"

Twenty Three

"**If** the internet is the new gold rush…sell shovels"

Twenty Four

"**Today**, reputation is everything...say what you do and do what you say"

Twenty Five

"**If** you don't help others...others won't help you"

Twenty Six

"**Trust** doesn't work…with people you don't trust"

Twenty Seven

"**Try** to do everything…and you'll do nothing"

Twenty Eight

"**Not** everyone is, or should be...an entrepreneur"

Twenty Nine

"**Great** ideas are allowed to be…simple ideas"

"**Stability** outside Ultrapreneurship…creates stability inside Ultrapreneurship"

Thirty One

Be HONEST
Even if others are not
Even if others will not
Even if others cannot

"He who walks honestly walks securely"
Proverbs 10:9

 Brotherhood of Christian Businessmen and Profession

"**Honesty** is the foundation…of the sustainable entrepreneur"

"**Network**…the Ultrapreneur's most valuable possession"

Thirty Three

"**Ignore** what people say…see what they do"

Thirty Four

"**Tame**...technology"

Thirty Five

"**Teach** what you know…to remember what to do"

"**Smell** the flowers on a regular…to help you keep it together"

Thirty Seven

"**Ensure** other's motivations...are in line with your aspirations"

Thirty Eight

"**If** your body is a temple...your business will be a fortress"

Thirty Nine

"**When** you have reason to give up…have more why you shouldn't"

"**Become** a master of…getting things done"

Forty One

"**Excellence** in…excellence out"

Forty Two

"**Innovators** create…Ultrapreneurs make it happen"

Forty Three

"**Business** is war but…Ultrapreneurship is love"

Forty Four

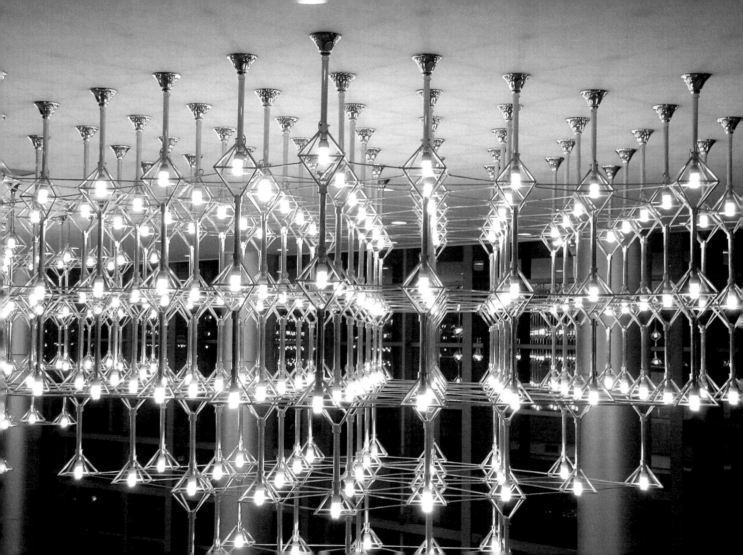

"**Ideas** are like opinions…everybody has one"

Forty Five

"**Network** now…with those you'll need then"

"**Success** is the Ultrapreneurial drug…get high"

Forty Seven

"**Burn** the bridge of failure...no going back"

Forty Eight

"**If** you don't act on your idea ...your idea will
act on someone else"

Forty Nine

"Don't 'Just do it'…if you don't know what you're doing"

"**Ultrapreneurship** will change your life…and maybe your friends"

Fifty One

"**You** can't do it alone…so don't even try"

"**Seek** out a mentor…then take their advice"

Fifty Three

"**If** cash is King…content is Queen"

Fifty Four

"**Don't** break the rules…follow them
then create your own"

Fifty Five

"**Avoid** admin… outsource, delegate, and automate"

"**Make** repeat business...your business"

Fifty Seven

"**Always** punch…above your weight"

Fifty Eight

"**Follow** your gut…not your MBA"

Fifty Nine

PERSONAL IDENTITY

"**Learn** from the successes of others…
but don't follow them"

"**Keep** your stuff in the cloud…and on the move"

Sixty One

"**Do** something for nothing…you might learn something"

Sixty Two

"**Live** off principle…profit will follow"

Sixty Three

Danger!

"**Business** with friends...exercise caution"

Sixty Four

"**To** grow online relationships…go offline"

Sixty Five

"**Balance** is the key…confidence the lock"

LEMONADE
5¢
Artificial light is measured
usually by foot candles(the
amount of visible light
striking an objest) and I am
perfectly willing to let the
manufacturers of such lights
give the instructions on how
they should be used. If
instructions are followed, as
to the distance the plants
should be for maximum
growth, you will not go far
wrong

"**The** best way to raise money...is to
raise it yourself"

Sixty Seven

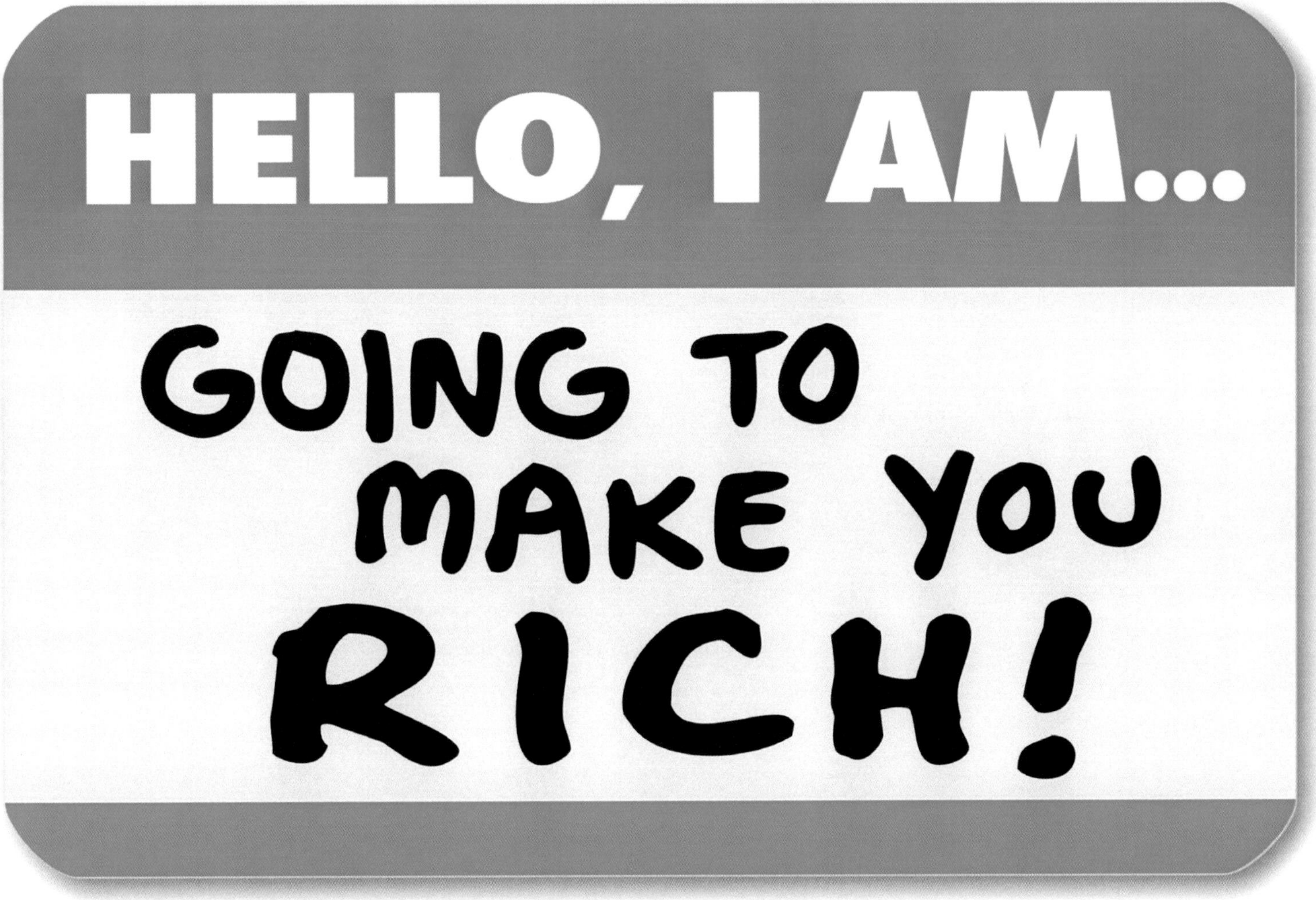
HELLO, I AM...
GOING TO
MAKE YOU
RICH!

"**Don't** let the internet...sell you a dream"

Sixty Eight

"You can start on a shoe string...just replace cash with excellence"

Sixty Nine

"**If** you only learn from your mistakes…work twice as hard to accommodate"

"**Don't** listen to your friends…listen to your customers"

Seventy One

"**Do** a little less…and over deliver"

Seventy Two

"**Good** ideas don't always make a…good business"

Seventy Three

1 + 1 = 2

"**What** makes you good at something...will make you good at something else"

Seventy Four

"**If** you're not motivated everyday...you're doing the wrong thing"

Seventy Five

"**Don't** be a…one hit wonder"

Seventy Six

"**You** can wake up…from a nightmare"

Seventy Seven

"**Measure**, learn…then react and act"

Seventy Eight

"**Get** the ball…out of your court"

Seventy Nine

"**Treat** investors' money…like it's your hard earned money"

"**Get** the support of family and friends…
then reward them with your dividends"

Eighty One

"**Study** other industries…do something new in yours"

Eighty Two

"**Caution:** Investors might turn you…into an employee"

Eighty Three

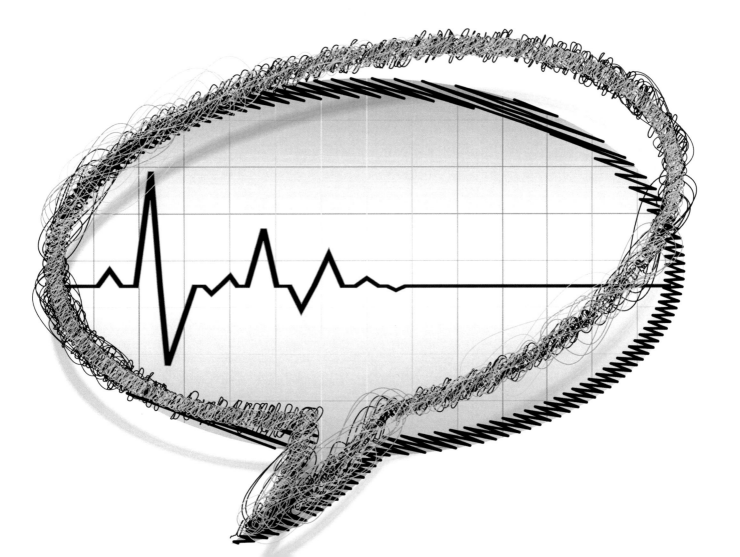

"**Current** affairs…will help you're sell your wares"

Eighty Four

"**Let** everyone know why you're…different"

Eighty Five

"**Remove** the weakest link...even if that means you"

Eighty Six

"**Yesterday's** solutions won't fix today's problems...in tomorrow's world"

Eighty Seven

"**Ok**, so you've done it once…do it again"

Eighty Eight

"**Make** your limitations…limitless"

Eighty Nine

"**Common** sense isn't common…assumptions are"

"**Genius** is…the Father of all invention"

Ninety One

"**Partner** with those…who have as much to lose as you"

"**Be** a great father, mother, husband, wife, friend, lover, brother, sister...one at a time"

Ninety Three

"**Fortune** is in the…follow up"

Ninety Four

"**Entrepreneurs** are leaders…just be careful where you lead them"

Ninety Five

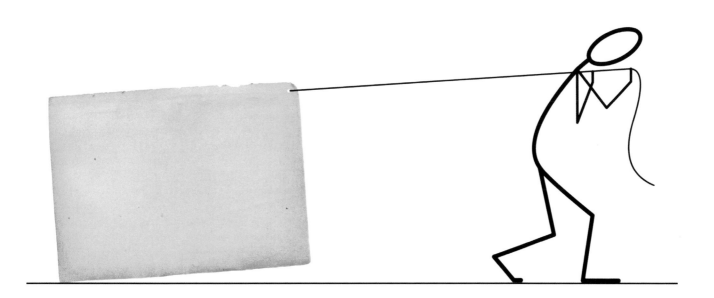

"**There** isn't a problem, being broke…won't make worse"

Ninety Six

"**Talk** only becomes action…with something to act-on"

Ninety Seven

"**Pivot** proactively…to protect your profits"

Ninety Eight

"**Is** entrepreneurship…the new religion?"

Ninety Nine

APPENDIX

The Art and Science of 'U' and 'You'

Ultrapreneurship represents an idea, captured visually as the gold and black "U" on the front cover of this book. That's the art bit. The science bit explains the meaning behind the images, colours and symbolism.

Let's go back to the definition of Ultrapreneurship: "A holistic approach encompassing all aspects of one's life including entrepreneurship, health and well being, family, spirituality, morality and mentality which come together to provide supreme balance."

The keyword here is 'supreme balance' which explains the colours used. The colour gold represents 'supreme', the colour black represents 'balance'. Together you have 'supreme balance'.

The familiar shape around the 'U' reminds us that we are only using a small portion of our minds. It reminds us that our potential is limitless and in some cases super human. We're all supermen and superwomen at times; we simply need to extend the ability we demonstrate during those times into the areas of our lives that need the most attention.

The letter 'U' represents both the word Ultrapreneur and the Greek letter μ pronounced Mu. This letter was derived from the Egyptian hieroglyphic symbol for water. And it is water that one must become like in order to succeed in Ultrapreneurship. The attributes of water which we can benefit from, as Ultrapreneurs, is its ability to adapt to any environment, go around any obstacle, remain pure but also absorb what's around it. Water can be a gentle, healing element but it can also be an unstoppable force, clearing everything in its path.

That's the art and science of 'U' and 'You'. This idea of unrealistic excellence that turns dreams into visions, visions into concrete plans and those plans into reality. In the end, it's this excellence that drives the contagious use of innovation which changes 'You', and the world, forever.

Credits

Jas Images – Front cover and book layout
Seraphim Media Agency – About the author image
Mutahir Mirza – Old building
Bruno E. Santos - Tank toy and yellow flowers
Henrik Sahlstrom – Ninja
Hersley Ven Casero – Be honest
Tanaki Alison - Music with Passion II
©Depositphotos /Pillar close-up@ arosoft
©Depositphotos /Artists painting palette@ bezikus
©Depositphotos / Stunt Biker. Free stile performing@ Mishella
©Depositphotos /Yin and Yang salt and pepper on old door@ sjhuls
©Depositphotos /Help message in a bottle@ jordygraph
©Depositphotos /Heart pulse@ marincas_andrei
©Depositphotos /Bulter with Call Bell@ scukrov
©Depositphotos /Polaroid instant camera@ Erdosain
©Depositphotos /Microphones on a table@ katatonia82
©Depositphotos /Tennis point@ jordygraph
©Depositphotos /Teaching@ xochicalco
©Depositphotos /Creating an idea@ Andreus
©Depositphotos /Polaroid instant camera@ Erdosain
©Depositphotos /Young handsome man with cracked face@ Moguchev
©Depositphotos /Zebras@ Webitect
©Depositphotos /Hello I Am Going to Make You Rich Nametag Sticker Money Wealth@ iqoncept
©Depositphotos /Lemonade Sign@ stevebonk
©Depositphotos /Gloomy woman in silver mask posing on a black
background.@ innervision
©Depositphotos /Lion Tamer with lion.@ ddraw
©Depositphotos /Pot of Gold@ truelight
©Depositphotos /Team of ants work with log, teamwork@ antrey
©Depositphotos /Shovel Surfing@ LuMaxArt
©Depositphotos /Surreal dark portrait of someone who's covering
his dirty face@ innervision
©Depositphotos /In a pursuit of profit@ Pixelery.com
©Depositphotos /Small plant growing@ mitarart
©Depositphotos /Young beautiful girl is professionally engaged in
yoga@ Nicknick_ko
©Depositphotos /DNA@ dnavarrojr
©Depositphotos /Smart schoolboy showing the mass-energy equivalence formula@ wavebreakmedia
©Depositphotos /Paradise tropical island in the form of infinity sign.
Infinite pleasure@ Space-kraft
©Depositphotos /Tiger and cat@ zhevelev
©Depositphotos /Memories of Ponte Vecchio@ fyletto
©Depositphotos /Opposite types of shoes@ AOosthuizen
©Depositphotos /Barcode fingerprint, vector@ beaubelle
©Depositphotos /Black and White Egg and Sperm@ GeorgesKyrillos
©Depositphotos /Samurai warrior@ sumners
©Depositphotos /Businessman sinking in heap of documents@ Nomadsoul1

"Ultrapreneurship...IS"

One Hundred